HANDWRITING COPY BOOK 2
JOINED WRITING

Peter Smith

Illustrated by Kate Shannon

A Piccolo Original
Piccolo Books

A note to parents

This book is designed to provide straightforward and fun activities for children from 7–11 years to practise joined writing and to develop a fluent and legible style of handwriting. The book covers (1) revision of print script (2) learning and practising joined writing (3) copying extracts and poems together with other varied activities.

There is no best method of handwriting, and since we hope the book may form a link between home and school, the style of writing used here has been carefully developed so that it should correspond closely to what is taught in the majority of junior and middle schools. It is intended to lead eventually to the development of an individual style based on good habits thoroughly mastered in the early stages, and may also be helpful for older children who wish to improve their handwriting.

We hope that the child will enjoy the activities and your role is crucial here. Encourage the child with praise and take the work in short spells so that interest and concentration don't begin to flag. Try to look at each page together and talk about it before the child attempts the activities – this will greatly improve understanding. There are parent notes to explain the relevance of the activities.

Before the child starts, make sure you have the following items available: pencils, pens and felt pens; extra writing paper and an exercise book to be a 'best book' in which the child can write favourite poems, stories etc in his or her 'best' handwriting.

Before you start, please read the notes on the alphabet below and on holding a pencil and posture on the inside back cover.

The alphabet

Here are examples of the alphabets we will be using in this book.

1 Print letters (revision):

a b c d e f g h i j k l m n o p q r s t u v w x y z

2 Letters for joining:

a b c d e f g h i j k l m n o p q r s t u v w x y z

3 Capital letters

A B C D E F G H I J K L M N O P Q R S T
U V W X Y Z

Introduction to joined writing

Here is an example of the joined writing to be used in this book:

The word dinosaur means 'terrible lizard,' but most dinosaurs were peaceful creatures.

Notice how joins are made from one letter to the next:

dinosaur means
↑↑ ↑   ↑ ↑   ↑↑↑↑

These joins are just like the up-strokes of the swings pattern.

Go over the swings pattern.

uuuu uuuu

Now fill the fish with swing patterns.

The print letters used in the next few pages have started to slope to the right. This is to help the child prepare for joined writing. See the inside back cover for a glossary of special terms used in this book.

Before you try to do joined writing yourself, be sure you can make all the print letters correctly. Remember to start at the correct place and move in the correct direction.

From the pattern uuu come u y

Look at the model letters, go over the dotted ones, and then write your own.

u y   u y   u y

Look at the model sentences, go over the dotted ones, and then write your own.

Buy butter for my bun
Buy butter for my bun

A fun run in the sun
A fun run in the sun

> On the following pages, the child will be asked to go over a pattern (or letter), then draw it on her own. She should always look closely at the model first, go over the feint pattern and then draw her own. She could also use tracing paper for a change.

Go over this pattern, then finish the row. Remember always to start at the top.

Go over these letters, and finish the row.

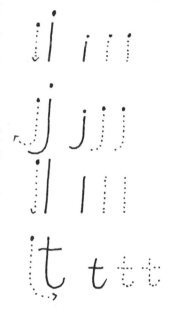

Copy the words below on a separate piece of paper and add one more of your own under each letter.

ice	jelly	lion	tiger
ink	jam	loaf	teapot
iron	joke	light	thumb
invent	jump	lady	tray
island	jewel	lord	train

These letters are all formed the same way – with a vertical straight line. Practising the straight line pattern (above) helps the child to form the letters i j l t correctly.

Go over the zig-zag pattern, then finish the row.

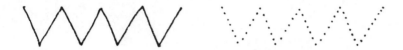

Go over these letters, then finish the row.

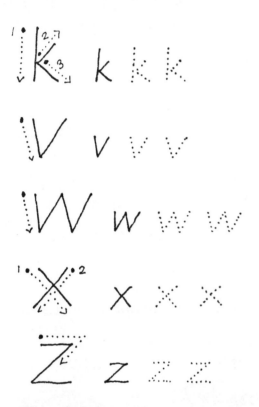

Go over this sentence, then copy it on a separate piece of paper.

We saw a fox, a yak and a zebra at the zoo.

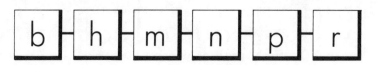

Go over the bridges pattern, then finish the row.

mm mmm

Go over these letters, then finish the row.

b b b b

h h h h

m m m m

n n n n

p p p p

r r r r

Look at these words:

ham pear bone bun pipe

Each word is written using only the six 'bridges' letters and the five vowels, a e i o u. How many words can you write using only these 11 letters? Write them carefully on a separate piece of paper.

Practise the 'c' pattern.

If you find it difficult to do, you can make a row of c's separately, but so close together that they touch, e.g. *ccccc*   But keep on trying to make the pattern this way:

Start at 1 and curve   up and over to 2   back and round again
back and round   from 2

Go over the letters, then finish the row.

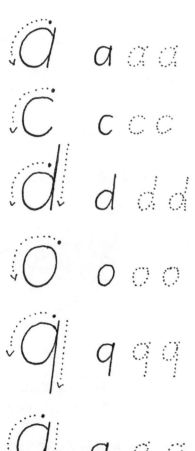

8

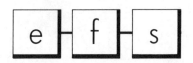

There is no simple pattern for these letters. Practise forming them by using the guide below.

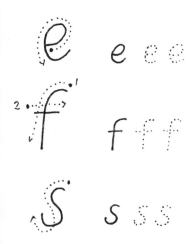

Can you work out this letter puzzle?

If even has two, eleven has three.
If fifty has two, fluffy has three.
If sense has two, sausages has three.

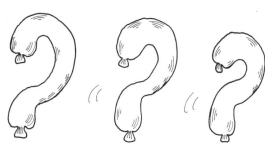

Can you think up some words which use two or more of the same letters?

Here are some words you will be coming across in this book. Make sure you can read and understand them. Then copy them carefully on a separate piece of paper.

bridges	pattern	vowels
capital	print	word
full stop	sentence	writing
join	space	zigzag
letter	swings	

Joined writing

Now that you have practised your print script, you can move on to joined writing.

To begin to join letters to each other, you should know these rules:

1 The letter k changes its shape. Instead of made in three separate parts, it becomes one: *k*

Here's how to write it correctly.

Start at 1 and come down to the bottom, then up again to 2.

from 2, go over and round and on to 3.

from 3, come down to 4.

Practise some 'joining k's'. *k k k*

2 We add a joining hook to the following letters. Finish the rows to practise the join.

a → a

d → d

h → h

i → i

l → l

m → m

n → n

u → u

10

The main join

Look closely at the joins in these sentences.

The skeletons of dinosaurs show that they were stupid animals. The very largest had a brain only the size of a hen's egg.

Most of the joins are based on the upward movement of the swings pattern and this is called 'the main join'.

Go over the swings pattern, then draw your own.

We use the main join to link a c d e h i k l m n t u

to any of these a c d e g i j m n o p q r s t u v w x y z

So 'a' joined to 'm' looks like this:

am uu
↖ main join ↗

Here are some examples of the main join to practise.

am
du
in
ho
ko
li
me
no
ta

Go over the swings and bridges pattern, then draw your own.

Now practise these main joins.

ac ac ac
cr cr cr
de de de
ed ed ed
hy hy hy
is is is
ko ko ko
ln ln ln
nm nm nm
ng ng ng

The 9 letters a c d e i m n t u can be joined together using the main join and without lifting your pencil.

Practise this.

acdeimntu acdeimntu

How many words can you make from these 9 letters only?

The second join

This is very similar to the main join and is used to link

a c d e h i k l m n t u to *b f h k l*

Practise this pattern.

ululul ululul

Here is how to do the second join:

ch   *ch*

As you finish the c continue straight up to the top of the h.

Then come straight down so that the c joins the h half-way up.

Practise these second joins.

ch ch ch
al al al
ll ll ll
ub ub ub
ck ck ck
if if if

Practise writing these words on a separate piece of paper:

church submarine swallow sack table truck

The third join

This is very easy. It is used to link $f o r v w$ to $a c d e g i j m n o p q r s t u v w x y z$

Here's how to do the third join:

$v + u = vu \qquad r + u = ru$

From the end of the v carry on to $\smile$, the beginning part of the u.

The little joining line $\smile$ should not be too long, and it can be slightly curved.

Practise these third joins.

ve ve ve

wa wa wa

or or or

rc rc rc

fi fi fi

va va va

ws ws ws

ot ot ot

Practise writing these words on a separate piece of paper. Notice how these use several examples of the third join:

river   fire   wok   work   sword
boot   forgot

The fourth join

Another easy one. It is used to link  and is really the same as the main and second joins.

Here's how to do the fourth join:

wl   rk   ob

The second join in each case is a natural link from the end of the first letter (1) to the beginning of the second letter (2).

The swings pattern will help you, so practise these patterns several times on a sheet of paper until you can do them well.

Now practise these fourth joins.

wh   wh   wh

rb   rb   rb

ok   ok   ok

of   of   of

Practise writing these words on a separate piece of paper.

wheel   joke   often   kerb

16

The break letters

Watch out! You don't need to make a join after these letters:

b g j p q s y x z

These are called 'the break letters'.

Look at these words. There are two 'breaks' in each.

bridge   stumble   pagan

Now copy these words several times and count the number of breaks in each word.

sailor
yesterday
apple
quick
lazy
brass
cabbage
major
squib
rubber
bandage
grumble

17

All joins with special attention to 'e' and 's'

Read these sentences, looking carefully at the way the joins are made. Pay particular attention to *e* and *s*.

When we do joined writing we should try to write smoothly and rhythmically. We should try to make the joins fluently and naturally. We should lift the pen only at break letters and the ends of words. It also helps if we sit properly and hold the pen correctly.

Look out! Did you notice that...?

- In *end*, the 'e' is made like this: *e*
- In *joined*, the 'e' is also made like this: *e* because an 'e' after a letter like 'n' has a diagonal bowl: *ne*
- In *break*, the 'e' is made like this: *e* because an 'e' after a letter like 'r' has a smaller bowl: *re*

- In *should*, the 's' is made like a print *s*
- In *easily*, the 's' is made like this: *s* because an 's' after a letter like 'a' has a pointed top: *as*
- In the word *letters*, the 's' is made like this: *s* because an 's' after a letter like 'r' has a flattened top: *rs*

Now copy out the sentences at the top of the page and take care with the joins. Look carefully at your writing and ask someone else to check it for you too. Keep practising if it's not quite right.

Capital letters

Capitals letters are easy. Just remember two things:

★ You never join capital letters
★ The capitals for joined writing are the same as for print except that they slope to the right.

Copy these letters.

Look at these words:

England Tom Betty Bath

Notice that the capitals aren't joined to the rest of the words. On a separate piece of paper write a place name or a person's name for each letter of the alphabet.

Make sure that the child understands that capital letters are only used at the beginning of sentences and for proper nouns, i.e. names and places. Try giving her a list of words and get her to write in the capital letters where necessary.

19

Practise pages

Read the poem. Notice how the joins are made, and the way the capital letters are not joined.

George's Pet

When George and his gorilla
Go bounding down the street,
They get respectful nods and smiles
From neighbours that they meet.

If George had owned a puppy-dog,
Or else a kitty-cat,
His neighbours wouldn't notice him
With courtesy like that.

Margaret Mahy

Copy out this poem carefully and then check over your writing.
Look particularly at:

★ the shapes of your letters
★ the joins

If you are not satisfied with what you have done – try again. Then write out the poem in your 'best book'.

> Encourage the child to keep a 'best book' in which she can carefully write out the passages on the following pages. She could also write out other favourite poems and extracts.

Read this extract from the story of Swan Lake then copy it carefully.

They soon came out on the shores of a lake and gazed in wonder, for there on the surface of molten silver glided the flock of white swans. How beautiful they looked - how sad too! And leading them was the whitest and most beautiful of them all, the swan with the golden crown.

When you have written this passage, look carefully at what you have written. Are you satisfied with:

★ the shape, size and spacing of the letters?
★ the shape and slope of the joins?
★ the spaces between the words and lines?

If not, write it out again and try to improve the things you were not pleased with.

Look at the picture of Robinson Crusoe and read this description of his clothes.

I had a great high shapeless cap, made of a goat's skin, with a flap hanging down behind to keep off the weather. I had a short jacket of goat-skin, the skirts coming down to the middle of my thighs, and a pair of open-kneed breeches of the same. The breeches were made of the skin of an old she-goat, whose hair hung down such a length on either side that, like pantaloons, it reached to the middle of my legs.

Now copy the passage carefully.
Check your writing and, if not satisfied, do it again and try to improve it.

Speed writing

Sometimes you will need to be able to write quickly, but remember, your writing must still be easy to read.

Try copying out this poem in your best handwriting. Get someone to time you while you do it.

My Sister

My sister's remarkably light,
She can float to a fabulous height.
It's a troublesome thing,
But we tie her with string
And use her instead of a kite.

Margaret Mahy

Look over your writing. Are the letters and joins correctly made? Now write the poem again as quickly as possible but making sure that it is still easy to read. Again, get someone to time you.

My sister's remarkably light,
She can float to a fabulous height.
It's a troublesome thing,
But we tie her with string
And use her instead of a kite.

Is your writing still easy to read and are the letters and joins correctly made? Now try to write the poem even more quickly . . .!

First read this passage from 'Pippi Longstocking' then copy it in your best writing. Get someone to time you.

Her hair was the same colour as a carrot, and was braided in two stiff pigtails that stood straight out from her head. Her nose was the shape of a very small potato, and was dotted with freckles. Under the nose was a really very large mouth, with healthy white teeth. Her dress was curious indeed, Pippi had made it herself. It was supposed to have been blue, but as there hadn't been quite enough blue cloth, Pippi had decided to add little red patches here and there. On her long thin legs she wore long stockings, one brown and the other black. And she had a pair of black shoes which were just twice as long as her feet.

Now see how much of this passage you can copy in three minutes. Remember it must be easy to read! Try this several times and see how your speed improves.

Draw Pippi in your 'best book'.

24

Writing and spelling

You can improve your spelling by practising writing groups of letters.

Look at this drawing, then copy each of the sets of words carefully. See if you can write them again from memory.

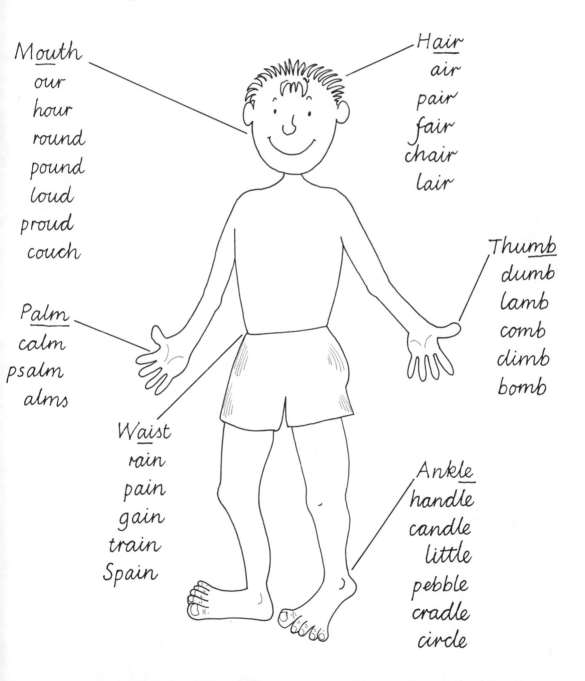

Mouth
our
hour
round
pound
loud
proud
couch

Hair
air
pair
fair
chair
lair

Palm
calm
psalm
alms

Thumb
dumb
lamb
comb
climb
bomb

Waist
rain
pain
gain
train
Spain

Ankle
handle
candle
little
pebble
cradle
circle

Now write a list of words with the same groups of letters for each of these parts of the body: KNEE ARM HAND BONE

25

The supermarket

Here is a list of food and drink you might find in a supermarket. Copy the list in your best writing and then see how many of the letters you can find three more items for. You will need to write smaller than usual.

COPY   OWN WORDS

A apples
B biscuits
C currants
D dates
E eggs
F fish
G garlic
H honey
I ice-cream
J jelly
K kidney
L lemonade
M marmalade
N nuts
O oranges
P peas
Q quiche
R rice
S sugar
T tea
U ugli
V vegetables
W wine
Y yoghurt
Z zabaglione

Can you find anything in a supermarket beginning or ending with the letter 'x'?

Palindromes

A palindrome is a word that reads the same way backwards and forwards.

For example redder becomes redder
　　　　　　　1 2 3 4 5 6　　　　　　6 5 4 3 2 1

Carefully copy this palindrome wheel and try to arrange the words to fit the wheel.

Can you find any other palindromes?

Here is a palindrome sentence.

Madam I'm Adam

Can you make up one?

27

Word chains

Here is a word chain:

adverb B *basic* C *could* D *decide* E *elf* F *farming* G *gash* H *harakiri* I [break 1] *junk* K *kneel* L *loom* M *melon* N *no* O *overlap* P [break 2] *quicker* R *roses* S *silent* T *tutu*

The chain is formed when the first letter of one word is the same as the last letter of the previous word. These are the 'link' letters and must be in alphabetical order. (There are two breaks in the chain because there are no words beginning with *i* and ending with *j* or beginning with *p* and ending with *q*).

Copy the chain in your best handwriting on a separate piece of paper.

Now use these words to form a chain from A to H.

dive growth bionic aplomb clawed flag elf

Is your chain in alphabetical order?
Is it neatly written?

If we add the words harmonica to the list we can form a circular chain from A to A.

A *aplomb* B *bionic* C *clawed* D *dive* E *elf* F *flag* G *growth* H *harmonica*

Now do the same with these words.

kennel laburnum modern no outstrip pink

Can you make up some chains of your own? See how long you can make them — start with any letter you like.

Use a dictionary to look up the words you don't know the meaning of.

Common sayings

Sometimes we say someone is 'down in the mouth' because they look miserable and we say someone 'stuck out their neck' when they took a chance. Here are eight sayings.

Her eyes were blazing.
His jaw dropped.
Down in the mouth.
Her ears were flapping.
She didn't bat an eyelid.
He stuck his chin out.
She's all mouth.
He sticks his nose in everything.

Do you know the meaning of each saying?
Now write the correct saying beside the drawing.

Draw your own pictures for the sayings not illustrated above.

Favourite foods

Copy out the poem below in your best handwriting.

What I like

What I like for dinner when I'm on my own
Is fish and chips, asparagus tips
And an ice-cream cone.

What I like for dinner when I have a guest
Is mossy fudge and muddy sludge
And baked bird's nest.

Margaret Mahy

Now, on a separate piece of paper, describe the meal you would like to give your friend. Check your writing for style and then copy it into your best book.

Read through this poem. Copy it out in your best handwriting and illustrate it with drawings.

The sleepy giant

My age is three hundred and seventy-two,
    And I think, with the deepest regret,
How I used to pick up and voraciously chew
    The dear little boys whom I met.

I've eaten them raw, in their holiday suits;
    I've eaten them curried with rice;
I've eaten them baked, in their jackets and boots,
    And found them exceedingly nice.

But now that my jaws are weak for such fare,
    I think it exceedingly rude
To do such a thing, when I'm quite well aware
    Little boys do not like to be chewed.

And so I contentedly live upon eels,
    And try to do nothing amiss,
And I pass all the time I can spare from my meals
    In innocent slumber - like this.

Charles Edward Carryl

Feelings

Here are two faces. One is happy but the other is sad. Below is a list of words. Write them out in your best writing in two lists to match the faces. If you're not sure of the meaning of a word, use a dictionary.

fear joy misery pleasure pain despair enjoyment satisfaction appreciation gloom anger depression suffering relief fright success horror contentment annoyance delight anxiety happiness resentment elation

When you have written your two lists, check that you have made the letters and joins well. Then write out your lists again but this time write each one in alphabetical order.